COLOUR MY

COLOUR MY

A VERY ADULT, ADULT COLOURING BOOK

BECKY GLASS

Copyright © Orion 2016

The right of Orion to be identified as the author
of this work has been asserted in accordance with
the Copyright, Designs and Patents Act 1988.

This edition first published in Great Britain in 2016
by Orion
an imprint of the Orion Publishing Group Ltd
Carmelite House, 50 Victoria Embankment
London EC4Y 0DZ
An Hachette UK Company

1 3 5 7 9 10 8 6 4 2

A CIP catalogue record for this book
is available from the British Library.

ISBN: 978 1 3987 0079 6

Printed in Italy

www.orionbooks.co.uk

INTRODUCTION

Stressed out? Full of rage? Work full of **WANKERS**? Are your kids behaving like little **PLONKERS**? Crappy commute?

Life can be tough and it's easy to find yourself curled up, screaming with anger and wanting to poke someone in the face with a pencil.

Well, prepare to save yourself from mental meltdown. Lower that crayon, aim it firmly at these pages and channel your angst into making something beautiful. Science*, research** and experts*** have proven that swearing as hard as you can pushes the brain to new heights of relaxation. **FUCK** meditation and yoga, there is no therapeutic method as effective at relieving tension than colouring in a big bold **UP YOURS, ARSEHOLE**! to the unavoidable onslaught of dirge dumped on us daily.

Now, deep breath. Don't reply to that email. Take a break from scrolling. Zone out from that sweaty person on the bus next to you. It's time to let go! **SOD IT**. Free yourselves! Accept that your partner is a **PILLOCK** and tell your boss to **BUGGER OFF**. As you colour in each page you will feel calmer, happier and, after the big finale, like a whole new person.

So get bloody well colouring in!

* / ** / *** The science, research and experts may not be real but who gives a shit?

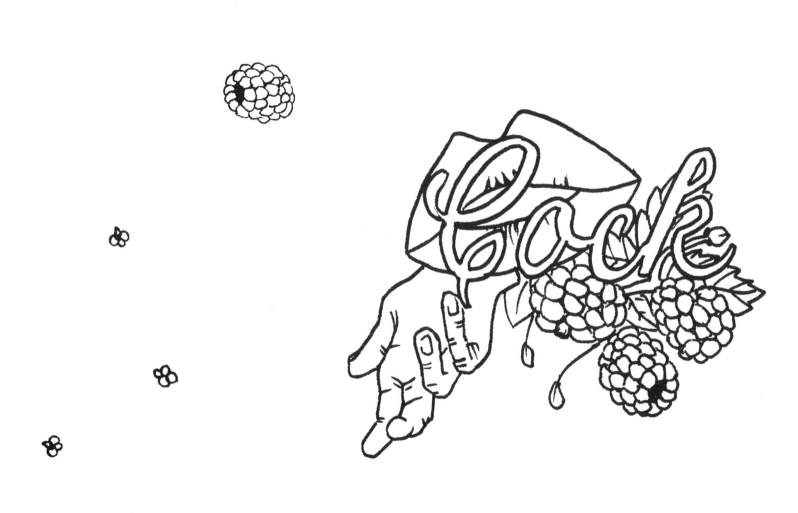

Do not turn over if easily offended . . .

Vent your rage and use these pages to create your own bloody swear words!